Kent Verses

Edited By Elle Berry

First published in Great Britain in 2018 by:

Young Writers
Remus House
Coltsfoot Drive
Peterborough
PE2 9BF
Telephone: 01733 890066
Website: www.youngwriters.co.uk

All Rights Reserved
Book Design by Ashley Janson
© Copyright Contributors 2018
SB ISBN 978-1-78896-410-4
Printed and bound in the UK by BookPrintingUK
Website: www.bookprintinguk.com
YB0359B

FOREWORD

Young Writers was established in 1991, dedicated to encouraging reading and creative writing in young people. Our nationwide writing initiatives are designed to inspire ideas and give pupils the incentive to write, and in turn develop literacy skills and confidence, whilst participating in a fun, imaginative activity.

Few things are more encouraging for the aspiring writer than seeing their own work in print, so we are proud that our anthologies are able to give young authors this unique sense of confidence and pride in their abilities.

For our latest competition, Rhymecraft, primary school pupils were asked to enter a land of poetry where they used poetic techniques such as rhyme, simile and alliteration to bring their ideas to life. The result is an entertaining and imaginative anthology which will make a charming keepsake for years to come.

Each poem showcases the creativity and talent of these budding new writers as they learn the skills of writing, and we hope you are as entertained by them as we are.

CONTENTS

Aycliffe CP School, Dover

Jefferson David Andrade (10)	1

Bedonwell Junior School, Belvedere

Isobel Boughwood (8)	2
Emily Goward (8)	4
Precious Feyishara Oyeleke (9)	5
Megan Grace Farr (8)	6
Bavanika Thirubavananthan (8)	7
Charlotte Weller (9)	8
Emma Mary Partridge (9)	9
Gladys Imisioluwa Odeyemi (9)	10
Riley Osborne (8)	11
Neha Patel (8)	12
Reese Sutton (9)	13
Navjot Singh Thumber (9)	14
Mobolaji Gamaliel Alo (9)	15
Sophie Bruzas (8)	16
Sophia Stapleton (8)	17
Anishka Arulnanthy	18
Leonardo Kim Long (8)	19

Blean Primary School, Blean

Theodora Wang (9)	20
Hugo Fassum (9)	21
Gabe Gill (8)	22
Isabella Wright	23
Aiyana Zarak Mirza (9)	24
Maisy Jackman (10)	25
Lois Wells-Furby (10)	26
Sienna Merkaj (10)	27
Paula Capo Gonzalez (9)	28

Chantry Community Academy, Gravesend

Jasmin Rahl	29
Nithin (8)	30
Emilija Puodziukaityte (11)	31
Hamna Perraiz (9)	32
Emilija Beinarovica (9)	33

Danson Primary School, Welling

Lola Bibby (9)	34
Rojin Yilmaz (10)	36
Millie Wilson (9)	38
Zahra Selfi (8)	40
Fariba Afsheen Fiona (9)	41
Sofia Julianna Guthrie (8)	42
Mai Greenhead (8)	43
Finley Tyler (8)	44
Millie Laming (9)	45
Edward Lee George (10)	46
Nimisha Chongbang (8)	47
Pranavi Devaraj (11)	48
Tabitha Selby-Boothroyd (8)	49
Prasiz Gurung (10)	50
Paris Smith (9)	51
Yuvraj Singh (8)	52
Sakina Ruzieva (8)	53
Bailey James Stevens (7)	54
Bailey Berry (9)	55
Chloe Corbett (8)	56
Daniel Fell (7)	57
Lukas Gurung (10)	58
Emily Coates (8)	59
Rianna Jade Mahoney (9)	60
Ashley Frimpong (9)	61

Phoebe Amarh (8)	62
Lucy Pack (8)	63
Evie Mawer (10)	64
Ashley Poulton (9)	65
Connie Elizabeth Barclay (9)	66
Fatma Hayrettin (10)	67
Yixin Liu (7)	68
Ani Kosherova (9)	69
Nancy Lin (9)	70
Ruby Rose Nancy Dale (10)	71
Poppy Spencer (8)	72
Samuel Ward (8)	73
Charlotte Galbraith (8)	74
Folu Oguntolu (8)	75

Downderry Primary School, Downham

Uriel Da Cruz (10)	76
Fola Oluokun (10)	78
Ty Johnson (10)	80
Ryan Johnson (8)	81
Aayushi Shrestha (9)	82
Evie Kielthy (11)	84
Bishman Karnan (11)	85
Asmitha Thayaruban (7)	86

Eastry CE Primary School, Eastry

Filipe Papadopoulos (8)	87
Imogen Elizabeth Cork (9)	88
Grace Lauren Welch (9)	89
Aidan Booth (9)	90
Harry Boakes (9)	91
Rhys Bagshaw (9)	92
Callum Roberts (9)	93
Logan Moor (9)	94
Flynn Goodrich (8)	95
Oliver Regan (9)	96
Freddie Silk (9)	97
George Clarke (8)	98
Joshua Kemp (9)	99
James Baker (8)	100

Edgebury Primary School, Chislehurst

Jeremiah Taylor (10)	101
Rose Acutt (9)	102
Erin Cole (10)	103
Megan Smart (9)	104
Evie Kouzaris (10)	105

Finberry Primary School, Ashford

Peggy Julia Barrett (9)	106
Maggie Mae McQuillan (8)	107
Jessica Slade (9)	108
Adra Louise Rothwell	109
Jonathan Osho (9)	110
Timotei Bilc (9)	111
Noah Foy (9)	112

Fleetdown Primary School, Dartford

Bethany Venn (8)	113

Hamstreet Primary Academy, Ashford

Iona Trigg (9)	114
Rhys Jones (9)	115
Zach William Rivett (9)	116
Megan Pettit (9)	117
Isla Jones (9)	118
Alex Tomlinson (9)	119
Ríona O'Neill (9)	120
Erin Eccles-Shorter (9)	121
Natalia Andreea Dragomir (9)	122
Erin Othen (9)	123
Fraser Henderson (9)	124
Matthew Baggaley (9)	125
Matilda Glancy (9)	126
Lucy Maddison (9)	127
Oscar Grant (9)	128
Lilly Santer (9)	129
Ben Smith (9)	130
Grace Praman (9)	131

Lily Smith (9)	132
Jaden Bailey Blunsdon (9)	133
Tom Dickens (10)	134
Sophie Eliza Ward (9)	135
Michaiah Asare (9)	136
Harry Body (9)	137
Jay Russell (9)	138

Hextable Primary School, Hextable

Naomi Akpomuje (10)	139
Scarlett Davie (9)	140
Chloe Green (9)	142
Emelia Anne Steele (10)	144
Alicja Jolanta Lechowicz (10)	145
Evie Whitlock Wilcox (9)	146
Lis Abdullahu (10)	148
Mia Penny (10)	149
Nell Regan (10)	150
Louisa Collins (10)	151
Elouise Sophie Waterton (10)	152
Alex Hills (9)	153
Maisie Olivia Brown (9)	154
Olivia Paige Stoyles (10)	155
Fiona Grace Horley (9)	156
Jack Hillam (10)	157
Sophia Stanton (9)	158
Dolcie Olivia Mae Couldridge (9)	159
Bridget Hancock (10)	160
Amy Morley (10)	161
Bradley Archer (10)	162
Lauren Bonnie Sawkings (9)	163
Maddie Vesey (9)	164
Millie Thompson (9)	165
Harrison Jacob Pyle (10)	166
Jack Nurthen (9)	167
Connor Martin George Bishop (10)	168
Archie Carroll (9)	169
Toby Cockerham (10)	170
Happy Grace Chikerema (9)	171
Oliver Moore (9)	172
Kelila Ogieva-Okunbor (10)	173
Joseph Bell (10)	174
Noah Frederick Leland Dawson (9)	175
Lily-Rose Bishop (10)	176
Charlotte Louise Sewell (10)	177
Keira Leigh Farnham (10)	178
Molly Chandler (10)	179
Lenny John Lewis (9)	180
Leo Baker (9)	181
Chloe Jones (10)	182
Herbie Holland (9)	183
Jacob Hick (9)	184
Tommy Hibbert (9)	185
Will Brazier (9)	186
Frankie Hibbert (9)	187

THE POEMS

A Poem About Love

My heart was empty until I found you,
You are my world, land, city
And you are also very pretty.

You shimmer like stars
And you're as valuable as diamonds,
You are my life, you're everything to me.

Your eyes are like pearls,
You complete me, like the ocean.

I wouldn't give you up for all the gold in the world,
I would die for you, I would live for you,
I would do anything for you.

Jefferson David Andrade (10)
Aycliffe CP School, Dover

Mermaids Love Candy

U nderwater is the best
N o human could ever live
D o not enter Underwater Mermaid Land
E very mermaid will survive
R un down to the water where you will see...
W ater is magical and will cool you down
A nything magical will change the day
T o survive you must wear goggles
E lsewhere you will die
R efreshers are the best candy.

M ermaids are the best
E veryone is fabulous
R ivers are dirty, seas are clean
M ermaids will help you survive
A t the bottom of the sea the magic begins
I nside a clam lives magical pearls
D own where they live candy is everywhere.

L and is good but water is better
A nyone can find a mermaid with candy
N o one can track a mermaid without candy
D o not even try!

Isobel Boughwood (8)
Bedonwell Junior School, Belvedere

Candy And Animal Land

C andy, all you can eat, a buffet of candy.
A nd cute animals, cuter than bunnies.
N o boring things, just fun things.
D o whatever you want to do, it's all up to you.
Y ou will meet animals and more magical creatures.

A nd you never get tired, or even bored.
N o bedtimes, just fun times are all you need.
I won't tell you what to do because you do what you want.
M ammals and reptiles and more you can see.
A nd all you get to do is chase them.
L oads of candy, come and see for some more.

L ands of candy and animals, what do you want?
A nd that's not it, all you've got to do is come and see.
N o more bullies, or rowdy ones.
D o what you can, no problem at all! Have no fear!

Emily Goward (8)
Bedonwell Junior School, Belvedere

Magical To My Ears

M ade-up animals can be fun
A nd crazy, nice to win and play with.
G igantic candies are also edible.
I would come to this world if I were you.
C andy, candy, yum in my tummy!
A lways eat it each day.
L eaving it will just be a heartbreak!

T oday will be my time and hour.
O ops, I meant my day and time...

M ake my day and come with me.
Y ou'll see me, you'll see me!

E lectronics are *not* allowed!
A ll you need are clothes in the tent.
R ead, shout, run about.
S o relax, eat candy, grab a unicorn and have fun!

Precious Feyishara Oyeleke (9)
Bedonwell Junior School, Belvedere

Books

Books, books
everywhere,
even piled up on the stairs.
Reading them under the covers at night,
going on adventures where werewolves bite,
underwater, overseas,
that's where I'd like to be.
All the faces I have seen,
all the places I have been.
Reading inside or outside,
I have laughed and I have cried.
Roald Dahl, JK Rowling and many others,
they've all become as close to me
as the Grimm brothers.
Magical adventures, romance and sci-fi,
poetry, jokes, all make my heart fly.
So pick up a book, give it a go,
oh, all the places you will go!

Megan Grace Farr (8)
Bedonwell Junior School, Belvedere

Possible Land!

Impossible is possible
in my Possible Land.
People have wings, but
won't have hands!

We have a flying kettle,
which is often hard to settle!
You can eat an invisible bun,
pitter and patter on the pinky sun!

Balls can talk,
they can even eat pork!
Houses can come alive and
they make good beehives!

Come in with impossibles,
so that my land can make it possible.
No need to fear,
because no one here has any tears.

My land is awesome!

Bavanika Thirubavananthan (8)
Bedonwell Junior School, Belvedere

The Beach

I can smell the saltwater air
and people eating fish and chips
and the crispy cod smells really nice.

I can feel the grainy sand in-between my toes
and the salty water flows through my hair
when I swim.

I can hear people having fun in the sea
and seagulls screeching high in the sky.

I can see the dogs splashing in the sea
people making sandcastles in the sun.

I can taste the salty, vinegary chips
and the crispy skin of the cod crunch in my mouth.

Charlotte Weller (9)
Bedonwell Junior School, Belvedere

Magical Unicorns!

A beautiful being, enchantingly pure,
as white as a lily, so proud and so sure.

With a silvery mane that flows in the breeze,
and eyes that bewitch you
and make your soul freeze.
But in an instant,
her eyes seemed to change and melt the ice,
causing feelings so strange.

Slowly the unicorn begins to shine,
gleam and glow,
for she is the meaning of good...
She reigns as queen in the mystical,
magical, enchanted wood!

Emma Mary Partridge (9)
Bedonwell Junior School, Belvedere

The Birth Of A Wondrous Unicorn

In the middle of the forehead grows a horn.

It's a riddle of the riddle,
who is born?

With a little, white, horse body,
a beard, just like a goat,
a lion's tail and hind legs,
like a graceful antelope.

A horn that spirals upward
from the middle of its head,
which begins in white and
then turns black and finally ends up red!
What is it?

The answer to the riddle is a wondrous unicorn!

Gladys Imisioluwa Odeyemi (9)
Bedonwell Junior School, Belvedere

Music Land

M usic is amazing.
U ndeniably, it's amazingly cool.
S ing anywhere and anytime.
I go to keyboard lessons, so you can come too!
C ello, guitar and drums are the instruments I play.

L ove the sound of music.
A fun, calm land full of music.
N o one will want to leave so come on!
D on't leave, come and play in our special hotel.

Riley Osborne (8)
Bedonwell Junior School, Belvedere

Sweety Sweety Candy

C andy is best thing ever
A lthough it can change the world!
N ever get rid of candy.
D o not enter the vegetables and fruit's land.
Y ou will be amazed by what you can eat in the

L and of candy.
A mazing stuff every day.
N ever, ever eat fruit, always eat candy.
D o not listen if your parents tell you to eat anything but candy!

Neha Patel (8)
Bedonwell Junior School, Belvedere

Rhyme Time

I really like to rhyme
I do it almost all the time.

I like to write a poem
it's what keeps me going.

If I am not making a rhyme
I'm usually squeezing a lime
sometimes, even playing a chime.

Now when I look at the time
I'm seeing if it's time to rhyme.

Why don't you try?
I'm not going to lie
it's quite fun!

Reese Sutton (9)
Bedonwell Junior School, Belvedere

This Is My Land

This is my land
You can make it expand,
You can make new friends,
Design the latest trends.

No one gets fined,
Unless they cross the line.

Everything is made of candy.
It really comes in handy!

There is lots of food,
Even if you're not in the mood.

Everything is magic,
Nothing is tragic.

Navjot Singh Thumber (9)
Bedonwell Junior School, Belvedere

Footy Land

In Footy Land,
rugby is banned.

We play football every day
but we don't play in May.

On the land
we have no sand.

We have soft grass,
so it's easy to pass.

We all have fun
in the sun.

So stop playing video games
and try to get some football fame!

Mobolaji Gamaliel Alo (9)
Bedonwell Junior School, Belvedere

Pet-Diamond Land

I can hear people laughing
and children opening their chocolate.
I can see yummy candy canes
and cute pets running around.
I can smell delicious chocolate
and smelly dogs running around.
I can touch beautiful diamonds
and yummy chocolate.
I love Pet-Diamond Land.

Sophie Bruzas (8)
Bedonwell Junior School, Belvedere

Weird Land

W elcome to Weird Land.
E very day
I t's full of weird things.
R un outside and see something different
D ay and night!

L augh out loud
A nd
N ext time see
D ifferent things!

Sophia Stapleton (8)
Bedonwell Junior School, Belvedere

Friendly World

In Friendly World
all is great.

For everyone's kind
with generous minds.

It is very homely
and no one is lonely.

No one is mean
but everyone is keen.

Friendly World
is the perfect world.

Anishka Arulnanthy
Bedonwell Junior School, Belvedere

Fizz

I feel cold cans of fizz, fizzing.
I like the houses, colourful and bright.
I like the taste of fizz fizzing in my mouth.
I like the sugary smell filling my nose.
I really love Fizz World.

Leonardo Kim Long (8)
Bedonwell Junior School, Belvedere

Forest Friends

Delve deep into a dream as you sleep,
Flowery fragrances fill the air.
Birds singing sweetly and grass growing neatly,
The chatter of squirrels in the trees.
Lush, green leaves above,
Gently swaying branches,
Tall, straight trunks of trees,
Crooked, rough trunks of trees.
Stream flows gently by,
Trickle of water and splash of fish.
The bushy, red-brown tail of a fox
Disappears among the foliage thick.
Dainty, white daisies with butterflies on top,
The soft buzzing of bees.
All too soon, the dream ends,
The forest dissolves,
The bedroom appears.

Theodora Wang (9)
Blean Primary School, Blean

Tree House Land

Tree House Land is very grand.
It's on the beach and is covered in sand.
Lots of builders planning creation
For towering houses through the nation.
Nobody lives in a house or a flat
But they do like walking in a very posh hat.
Everything is expensive
A lovely place to live.
You would like to be there
Even though everything is in the air.
Ladders leading up to every home
Some people make friends
with their garden gnome.
Now that is all I have to say
About this land that is far away.

Hugo Fassum (9)
Blean Primary School, Blean

Sweet Nightmares

One cold and bitter night
I heard a noise that
Gave me a fright
A wicked candy came.

He was not what I thought a
nice sweet would be like.
He was in fact a wicked guy.
He brought bad bellies and tooth decay!

Worse was Mr Chocolate Sugar.
Yummy, creamy...
Making me fat.

Flying around was a jelly bat,
Oh, stop the nightmare!
Mummy, I promise I'll eat my
carrots, so they can't get me
In the dark!

Gabe Gill (8)
Blean Primary School, Blean

The Land Of Silver

Where the grass is pearly white
and the flowers are silver-blue.
The sun shines like a ring and
a pearl looks like the moon.

The castle is silver with pearly spikes,
the royal family have silver eyes.
The wolves in the silver forest
have feet that sound like bells.

Where the grass is pearly white
and the flowers are silver-blue,
I go there in my dreams,
maybe you do too?

Isabella Wright
Blean Primary School, Blean

Dreams Come True Land

My land is pure, my land is gold
My land is sunny, my land is cold
Green meadows, blue lakes all around
Playing children, working parents all around
The land that welcomes all that want to stay
The land helps all those who go astray
None are more or less important
Deeds, not words, are important
We play and work hard in this land of ours
We seek treasures and riches in this land of ours.

Aiyana Zarak Mirza (9)
Blean Primary School, Blean

In Space

In space, where grass doesn't grow
and everywhere you pass,
you see plants flashing past!

In space, where no one goes,
are some planets, still unknown.

In space, where I've never been
and there's no air,
but some places are still out there.

Maisy Jackman (10)
Blean Primary School, Blean

Harry Potter World

This wonderful world of wizardry
The perfect wizardry world
The world of quidditch and potions and spells
Goblets of fire and orders of the phoenix
With Snape and Voldemort
The wand, oh so delicate
With its intricate design
This wonderful world, I wish was mine.

Lois Wells-Furby (10)
Blean Primary School, Blean

Spells

S pells, spells, magical spells.
P laying with magical spells.
E xciting spells to learn.
L earning serious spells.
L oving spells all around me.
S aving my spells for another day.

Sienna Merkaj (10)
Blean Primary School, Blean

Uni-Land

All I see are unicorns around me,
Grazing in the moonlight.
Magic whizzing around in the air.
Unicorns roaming around, below, in the valley.
Unicorns shooting stars out of their horns.

Paula Capo Gonzalez (9)
Blean Primary School, Blean

My Favourite Candy Land

In my land there are...

Different types of trees.
One's made out of lemon drops,
that make you feel at ease.
Succulent, strawberry gum, my favourite,
just pick it off the bush,
it will be a craving.
I just hope that I'm not dreaming.
Gummy pens you can even write with.
I'm just hoping that I'm not telling you myths!
Sultana Superman, flying through the sky.
"Do you want a ride?" he said.
"Yes please, but not so high."
Chocolate grass, yum, so good.
There's even a chocolate waterfall
where you can dip in food.
I love candy and so do you!

Jasmin Rahl
Chantry Community Academy, Gravesend

Imagination

I ncredible country to live in.
M ake your life amazing
A nd have a good imagination.
G reat day, great fun!
I t is amazing to use your imagination.
N ever be grumpy.
A ll the time, think up new worlds.
T o get new things.
I ncredible stuff!
O nly be good in the New World.
N ever fight!

Nithin (8)
Chantry Community Academy, Gravesend

Candy Land

I live in Candy Land,
where everything is so grand.
It tastes so good,
nothing is made of wood.
Lollipop trees,
marshmallow bees,
Candy cane bridge,
there is no need for a fridge.
Cotton candy clouds,
surrounded by crowds.
Enjoy the sweet,
don't eat the beets.
So come to Candy Land,
where everything is so grand.

Emilija Puodziukaityte (11)
Chantry Community Academy, Gravesend

Candy World

C andy canes as trees.
A ero as flowers.
N ever-ending candy rain.
D rizzling chocolate falls.
Y orkie rocks.

W agon Wheel treetops.
O reo cookie clouds.
R eese's sand.
L ion bars, as you guessed it, as lions!
D ang, I wish I could tell you more, but that's all!

Hamna Perraiz (9)
Chantry Community Academy, Gravesend

The Perfect Land

My little land would be fair
and they'd have the best mayor.
Plus her name would be Claire.
She'd share with all the lovely bears.
But a cat despised the bears
so decided to be a brat.
The cat and a rat
took the bears' mat,
But luckily, they didn't get his hat.
The bunny saw it all
and thought it was a bore!

Emilija Beinarovica (9)
Chantry Community Academy, Gravesend

Underwater World

When seagulls were putting on lotion
There was a huge commotion in the ocean.
A grand ship started sailing
And upon it, the captain started wailing.
"Look, look! There's my wish, 101 fish!"
A silly sailor announced a cod was a fish.
The hungry sailor added, "A very nice dish."
Meanwhile, Underwater World was ecstatic.
Cars started beeping, frogs started leaping
And babies started screaming at the ship's deck, which was gleaming.
Underwater World was very busy
And the drinks were extremely fizzy.
Moreover, there were traffic jams
And mums pushing babies in prams.
There were also green and purple streets,
But strangely no feet.
Tails not toes, swimming costumes not clothes,
Blue bees under turquoise trees.
In addition, there were reverberating sounds
And like archaeologists, there were things to be found.

Unlike us, there was a king sea louse
and the queen lived in an extraordinary house.
There were pink and blue cars, even yellow guitars.
So do you like the sound of it?
Why not come and visit?
PS, I guarantee when you leave, you'll miss it!

Lola Bibby (9)
Danson Primary School, Welling

Twinkle Land

In Star Land
you hold a star in your hand.
Stars as bright as the sun
at night are hung.

The bright moon
will rise soon,
but don't worry,
the stars will be there too!

Morning time is here,
children from their windows peer,
just to see the stars are gone.
Are the stars dead? Oh no they aren't!
They are in the sky, fast asleep!

The next night,
the shining stars are in sight.
Peekaboo!
Watch out, the moon can see you.

What's that in the sky, a shooting star?
Well, that's new, if I make a wish will it come true?

Millions of stars dancing in the moonlight,
Wow what a sight! Blinding light!

As the sky changes from black to blue,
the stars, one by one, will lose their twinkle.
But let me make this clear,
do not worry my dear,
do not fear,
as it will soon be a new day and a new night.

So hold onto your blanket tight,
dim the light and sleep tight.
Do not forget you are the queen of the night,
And won't give up until you put up a fight!

Rojin Yilmaz (10)
Danson Primary School, Welling

Harry Potter World

H ogwarts
A school of witchcraft and wizardry
R owling is an amazing author
R eading the Harry Potter series is adventurous and amazing
Y ears of Harry Potter magic.

P rivet Drive, number four
O rder of the Phoenix, book 5.
T ournaments of quidditch
T wist and turns on Harry's broomstick, 'Nimbus 2000'
E xperiments mixing magical potions and casting magical spells
R avenclaw, Hufflepuff, Slytherin and Griffindor.

W easley kids; Fred, George, Bill, Charlie, Percy, Ron and Ginny.
O rdinary Muggles also become witches and wizards.
R on, Hermione and Harry, BFFs.
L ongbottom; Neville! One of Harry Potter's close friends.
D umb Dursleys hated Harry Potter!

Millie Wilson (9)
Danson Primary School, Welling

My Land Of Dance

Land of Dance is a beautiful place,
I laugh, keep fit and learn at my own pace.
What is that I can hear?
Is that the beats of music to my ear?

Plié, chassé and bar work in ballet lessons.
It is over so quickly, and onto the next session!
With stretches, twists, jumps and turns,
I hop, skip and leap as I learn.

I perform at the theatre and compete on stage,
You have to be confident, no matter your age.
I've made lots of friends along the way
And cannot wait to dance on those special days.

It's thanks to my teacher for all that she's done.
She makes me love dance even more and have fun.
I love to visit my Land of Dance!

Zahra Selfi (8)
Danson Primary School, Welling

Nightmares In My Life

Nightmares sneaking in my bed,
living life over my head.
Causing all the fear to come alive,
bringing back memories with such a drive.
In them, someone is always after me,
why can't they let me go and let me be free?
Afraid to go to sleep at night,
they will start to cause such a fright.
The nightmares won't just go away,
in my sleep, they still betray
feelings that are buried deep down,
when I go to sleep they come around.
My mind, my life, I thought I'd freed them,
what I think is behind me will always stem.
Come and visit this place,
where you can suffer your face.
So when I go to bed I'll pray,
that I can sleep tonight till day!

Fariba Afsheen Fiona (9)
Danson Primary School, Welling

In Unicorn World

In Unicorn World, the sky is always blue
and there's nothing you can't do.
In Unicorn World, there's rainbows everywhere
and unicorns with glittery, colourful hair...

In Unicorn World, the food is candy,
In Unicorn World, the floor is never sandy.
When you touch the unicorns,
you'll get glittery hair,
just because the unicorns want to play fair.
But when day turns to dusk,
you have to say goodbye
but surely, in Unicorn World,
there's always a next time?
If you ever want to get there
jump through a keyhole and see what you find.
Unicorn World, a place that's divine.
You'll never want to leave, you just wait and see!

Sofia Julianna Guthrie (8)
Danson Primary School, Welling

Snowflakes And Candy

S now is white and also bright.
N ow it's time to play.
O ut come the hats, scarves and gloves.
W inter is so much fun.
F rozen puddles can be cracked.
L aughter fills the air as we chase each other
A s we stomp, our footprints through the snow.
K eep away from the pond, it's iced over.
E veryone likes a cup of hot chocolate
S nug and warm indoors.

C andy is so delicious.
A bit of it won't do.
N ever eat too much.
D id you ever live with the Gingerbread Man?
Y ou will love to live with us!

Mai Greenhead (8)
Danson Primary School, Welling

Dino Candy Land

D inosaurs weren't actually made of flesh
I n fact, they were made of candy!
N ot a speck of bone to be found.
O n the ground is not grass, but yummy worms.

C andy here and candy there.
A T-rex is made of cream,
N othing is not candy.
D angerous? No. Triceratops are made of Polos.
Y es, scientists are sure!

L ollipops make up an allosaurus,
A stegosaurus is made of chocolate.
N ext, when the asteroid hits, humans, we will eat it in bits.
D elicious dinosaurs are now no more!

Finley Tyler (8)
Danson Primary School, Welling

Nightmare Forest

Ghosts are flying through the air,
this is giving me quite a scare!
Spiders are messing up my hair,
this is turning out to be a nightmare!
Zombies are coming out of the ground
and they're pulling me down, down, down.
Vampires are getting close to my neck,
am I in the right place? I'll check!
Gargoyles are climbing up the walls,
I really, really, really want no more.
Bats are hiding in the trees,
I'm very nearly down on my knees.
Pumpkins are jumping out at me
and I really want to flee...
Argh!

Millie Laming (9)
Danson Primary School, Welling

Snow World

In my Snow World, all it does is snow,
Surrounded by mountains where we climb, then go.
In my wooden house with Dr Drake and woffeee,
I'm thinking of getting a cat
And calling it Moshee
We have an achievement room nearly very full
We camped up a mountain once, very tall.
Sometimes there are snowstorms, but we stay safe
In our wooden house with Dr Drake.
We like to camp a lot of the time
And we would *never* commit a crime.
There is nothing in our world that gives us a fright,
I love my Snow World, day and night.

Edward Lee George (10)
Danson Primary School, Welling

The Lost City Of Atlantis

Deep down in the dark, blue sea
there are creatures that have never been seen.
They lurk in the ruins of buildings, once ours.
Statues of gods who live in the stars
scattered along the ocean bed,
those ancient temples wildly spread,
hidden in the corners of the mystical lost city
There's caves filled with gems of high quality.
This is no place for a human to be,
as the creatures will hunt you violently.

Many tell a tale of a place like this,
but no one has ever come close to
the lost city of Atlantis.

Nimisha Chongbang (8)
Danson Primary School, Welling

Upside Or Downside?

On the Earth, shooting stars
are actually lights from cars
that are going 99 mph,
which is reckless, silly and plain sour.

In Upside, (or is it Downside?)
everything is the opposite to the surface
of the Earth.

On the Earth, stars
are actually lit up signs for bazaars,
that are filled with people,
as many as a street full!

In Upside, (or is it Downside?)
everything is the opposite to Earth,
that has not a flaw.

Everything is awesome,
In Upside, (or is it Downside?)

Pranavi Devaraj (11)
Danson Primary School, Welling

Duck World

D ucks are cute and fluffy.
U sually, ducks live near lakes.
C uddling them is lots of fun.
K ind people feed the ducks bread.
S ome ducklings can swim when they're only a year old.

R eally adorable ones waddle right up to you.

G ood ducks feed and love their babies.
R acoons are nothing compared to ducks.
E xcellent ducks can swim for hours.
A mazing ones are sometimes red or even purple!
T he best animal in the world is surely a duck.

Tabitha Selby-Boothroyd (8)
Danson Primary School, Welling

Cake Wars

C erium for exchanging at every teams' generators.
A ll cakes defended with towering brick walls.
K unzite being robbed from opposing teams.
E merald is being collected for diamond armour.

W hat's now happening throughout the map, as teams get eliminated?
A qua team now entirely out of the game.
R unners increase their speed to devour opposing teams' cakes.
S carlet team's cake now scoffed by intruders, (the yellow team), as the last few people surrender!

Prasiz Gurung (10)
Danson Primary School, Welling

Candylicious

C andylicious is crunchy and sweet and oh so neat.
A mazingly tasty and scrummy in my tummy.
N aughty but nice.
D elicious and colourful.
Y ummy, but also scrumptious.
L ickable and chewable.
I ncredibly sour and sugary.
C olourful and delightful, amazingly brightful.
I ndeed, it's addictive.
O h so different to anything else.
U tterly pleasant in so many ways.
S o here's Candylicious explained in many different ways!

Paris Smith (9)
Danson Primary School, Welling

Dinosaurs

Dinosaur here, dinosaur there.
Here come the dinosaurs,
they're everywhere!
They are so tall that when
you see them they say "boo!"
The dinosaurs are friends with me and you!

Dinosaurs here, dinosaurs there,
Everywhere you go, they are always there.
All they do is fill the air and sing,
The dinosaur song which is what they bring.

Dinosaurs here, dinosaurs there.
While they eat,
I'm always there
to find out,

Then write about!

Yuvraj Singh (8)
Danson Primary School, Welling

Magical Moor

M agic floats through the air.
A ll is peaceful everywhere.
G oing to the land of wonder.
I 'm sure I couldn't be fonder.
C hildren play without a care.
A lake of happiness is over there.
L ittle cuties that make up Magical Moor.

M ore phenomena every second.
O h, with a glamorous sound, unicorns beckon.
O ld, horrific memories drift away in my mind.
R ight now I am unique, one of a kind!

Sakina Ruzieva (8)
Danson Primary School, Welling

Candy Land

Candy Land is full of sweets.
I can't decide what to eat.
Down Candy Lane there is a chocolate train,
filled with jelly beans and yummy lollies.
It rains sherbet, so bring your brollies!
Be careful what you eat,
not everything tastes so sweet.
They might be pretty flowers,
but really, they are candy sours.
Be careful at night, it is dark,
watch out for the gummy shark.
Snakes and spiders made from jelly,
don't let them get in your belly!

Bailey James Stevens (7)
Danson Primary School, Welling

Nightmare Land

In this nightmare
you'll get a horrific scare.
Evil witches fly around
and to warn you, there's a terrible, piercing sound.

Petrifying monsters live in caves
and a Minotaur lurks in the middle of a maze.
At 3am, Charlie-Charlie comes out,
by the way, he'll haunt you if you shout.

You get alien homework every day
and triple alien school in May.
In this disastrous land,
chocolate, (my favourite), is banned!

Bailey Berry (9)
Danson Primary School, Welling

Candy Enchanted Forest

Have you ever wanted a land full of candy?
Well think no longer, because it's finally arrived!
Walking in the streets,
you see pink candyfloss as clouds
and giant lollies as trees.
The air smells as sweet as the land tastes.
The streets are Smarties
and flowers are M&Ms.
Strawberry laces for sticks that lay on the ground
and gingerbread houses for homes.
At the end, there is a huge rainbow to enter
another land...

Chloe Corbett (8)
Danson Primary School, Welling

Candy World

C andy World has a lot of candy
A nd it is an enjoyable place.
N ice people live in Candy World.
D id you ever think you could go to a place like this?
Y ou will have a great time!

W ell, this sounds amazing.
O n the top, you will have a great time as well.
R eptiles that are here, are lovely.
L ions are very lovely here.
D ig up as much candy as you need!

Daniel Fell (7)
Danson Primary School, Welling

The Funtastic Fun Park

Come to my fun park where fun is its name,
fun things all over the place,
fun rides, fun games and even fun spooks,
change your frown upside down
with a fantastic game.

This is your zone with fun shoved in,
the fun never stops, so I enter in.
The fantastic fun park will never end,
try and you'll never let go.
The fantastic fun park is at your click,
so what are you waiting for? Go, have fun!

Lukas Gurung (10)
Danson Primary School, Welling

Land And Sea

My world is made of land and sea.
Where lots of creatures like to be.
Dolphins, sharks and pufferfish
love to swim around.
Tigers, giraffes and polar bears search for food.
Elephants like to stomp about
with their huge feet on the ground.
They grab lots of leaves as they pass every tree.
Dolphins clicking and clacking
as they swim in the sea.
My world is the most fun of them all!

Emily Coates (8)
Danson Primary School, Welling

Candy Land

C andy Land is great!
A pples covered in toffee are cool.
N everland Castle is full of gummy bears.
D odgeballs are made out of peppermints.
Y o-yo city has great cola bottles.

L iquorice whips are skipping ropes!
A nd candy is tasty.
N othing tastes better than juicy, fruity sweets.
D on't leave Candy Land!

Rianna Jade Mahoney (9)
Danson Primary School, Welling

Candy Town

Marshmallow marshes and gumdrop trees,
chocolate bunnies and gummy bees.
Doors made of s'mores and streets of sweets,
such bittersweetness falls within
a candy-coated dream.
The place where hope extends
beyond the sugar-coated scheme.
Pools of such wonderfully pure sweetness,
swings made of pure goodness.
You'll never feel down when you're in Candy Town.

Ashley Frimpong (9)
Danson Primary School, Welling

Sweet Riddle World

In Sweet City, everyone's sweet,
if you're not, you don't get a treat.
When the sun comes down
and the rain comes in,
people doubt the sweets will go.
But the sun fights its way through
most of the mist
I'm bright once again, Sweet City exists.
If you ever wander to Sweet City,
don't buy a treat,
for they are filled with something gritty!

Phoebe Amarh (8)
Danson Primary School, Welling

Gymnastic Land

G ymnastic land
Y ou're always grand
M e and you have
N o shoes
A beam is smaller
S o you are taller
T hat bar is higher, but
I have only been on lower
C an do a cartwheel after?

L eotards we wear
A nd badges we like
N o boys allowed like
D avid and Mike.

Lucy Pack (8)
Danson Primary School, Welling

Cake Town

In Cake Town,
no one has a frown.
Strawberries and cream
make it like a dream.

Everyone likes cake,
it is really fun to bake.
You can make all different shapes and sizes,
which make fun surprises.

It's all made out of cake,
except the chocolate lake.
It's like a chocolate fountain
that runs down from the mountain.

Evie Mawer (10)
Danson Primary School, Welling

Candyfloss Heaven

In Candyfloss Heaven,
everything is from Devon.
Nothing is bland,
it's not even canned.

From apple to pear,
everything's fair.
It's pink and fluffy,
like a puppy.

It's sugary and sweet
and everything is neat.
Come to Candyfloss Heaven,
where it's well and truly Heaven.

Ashley Poulton (9)
Danson Primary School, Welling

Snow And Ice

I love the snow
It really does show
On the trees
With the sun on the leaves
It twinkles with the breeze

I love the ice
It rhymes with spice
If I could ski
I would go *whee!*

I love to skate with my best mate
I had to stop, because we hit the gate
We both agreed that was great!

Connie Elizabeth Barclay (9)
Danson Primary School, Welling

Holiday In A Dream

I can see boats from afar,
I can see fishermen,
trying to catch fresh fish,
to sell to make a living.
I see babies and kids playing on the sand,
I feel the light breeze whistle by
whilst lying on my sunbed.
I hear Mum calling, then I realise,
it's only a dream!

Fatma Hayrettin (10)
Danson Primary School, Welling

Magic Land

M agic cats.
A nimals.
G orillas eating bananas.
I like floating around.
C akes flying around without permission.

P erfect, beautiful pool.
O ctopus inside the pool!
O rangutan's fight with magic.
L ollipops flying around!

Yixin Liu (7)
Danson Primary School, Welling

The Little Lion Cub

The little lion cub,
as small as a cup.
At his birth he was left,
no food, no bed.

The little lion cub was nearly shot,
by the poachers who run along
with their gun so strong.

Yet the little lion cub
could not survive the wild
and by two weeks,
he was gone!

Ani Kosherova (9)
Danson Primary School, Welling

Candy Land

In Candy Land,
Everything is made from sweets,
so you can all eat.
Everyone gets cavities,
even all the gummy beans.

Why not come to this fun land,
Where you can join the candy band?
So stuff your faces
with the Skittles race.
Come and visit
and enjoy!

Nancy Lin (9)
Danson Primary School, Welling

Our World Of War And Peace

In our world,
there is good and bad.
In our world,
there is war and peace.
When we were born,
we were forced to choose.
Are we to win,
or are we to lose?
To change it all,
our dreams are in the bin.
In our world,
there is you
and there is me...

Ruby Rose Nancy Dale (10)
Danson Primary School, Welling

Candy Land!

There was once a land called Candy Land,
where all kids' dreams came true!
Full of treats and lots to eat
and sweets for me and you.
Chocolate lakes and strawberry flowers,
sounds crazy but it's true!
So come along to Candy Land
and you will love it too.

Poppy Spencer (8)
Danson Primary School, Welling

Dinosis

D o you dare come to Dinosis?
I s it really worth the risk?
N o, definitely not!
O n the island lie dangerous dinosaurs.
S o they will be waiting on the shores.
I nnocent though you plead.
S ome lucky people are freed.

Samuel Ward (8)
Danson Primary School, Welling

Dream Land

D reams come true in my land.
R ainbows everywhere!
E xciting things happen every day.
A nimals galloping around in the clouds.
M y world is very magical, it's the best place to be!

Charlotte Galbraith (8)
Danson Primary School, Welling

Dragon World

D angerous and furious creatures.
R elentless winds in my world.
A gile scales on the dragons.
G reat wings and teeth.
O verwhelming power and eyes.
N ice characteristics.

Folu Oguntolu (8)
Danson Primary School, Welling

Risk The Chance

I can't bear to look at the shape of the pixel.
Now it is a blur, is it something so simple?
All of the blocks, they're just an illusion
how can this game be such a confusion?
I think of the past as I lie in bed
and the only colour is my sword, stained red.

The trees and the grass,
they are all black and white,
all I can see is the light of the night.
The smoke is so thick, it's truly unnatural,
whenever I blink, it turns into nightfall.
The enemy are trampling miserable snow,
I stare at the ceiling, thinking, *I'll die tomorrow!*

They won't go away - an automatic update,
clouds, so grey they make me stay up late.
Murky water in the sticky swamps
that holds some secret for me to unlock.
The stories of this depressing world
are nothing like what you've been told.

So here we go into this adventure,
but beware, this is a dangerous venture!
The cabin is below the surface lightless,
the more you explore, the more you feel rightness.
The dirt is sharp, the air is baneful
and the splinters from the trees are truly painful.

I wish for you not to come across,
you might miss the chance; then have a loss.
A loss of your life, or a loss of your sanity,
or, as you wield your knife, the loss of humanity...

Uriel Da Cruz (10)
Downderry Primary School, Downham

Creeper Infestation

It lurks around in the shadows of the night,
It tickles my neck, giving me a fright.
It blocks my escape route, leaving me stranded,
I look around for help, but I realise I'm abandoned.

This monster's left me powerless,
with nowhere to go,
The only items I have are arrows, but sadly no bow.
I then hear a hiss sound behind me,
striking me with fear,
But when I turn around,
it's gone and disappeared.

I look around once more,
watching a blur of green and black,
I think to myself, *I thought it had disappeared!*
But once I realised it was here,
my mood instantly sank.
But what I saw next left me so blank.

It was robbing the village; taking the crops,
I was unable to defend — I was left to sobs

As I thought of what this creature was,
I could only think, *monster!*
But it revealed its identity and I recognised it:
the creeper!

Fola Oluokun (10)
Downderry Primary School, Downham

My Funland

My place is a huge, wonderful land.
Everywhere is either candy or sand.
The tall, waving trees are scattered
around the beach and in the centre
of the glowing island is a golden peach.
Everyone in the town is generous and kind,
plus, in the candy cane mansion you'll find
diamond statues, Oreo walls,
but you must look out for the sand trapdoor falls.
If you fall, you will fall for miles,
then when you reach the ground, there are piles
of fun things, like games
and smoothies and music galore!
When you are finished, you're going to want more!
As always, there are ships in a caramel sea,
no rats, no bugs, nothing annoying you'll see.
Every day is a holiday and a weekend too,
in my land, there is nothing you can't do!

Ty Johnson (10)
Downderry Primary School, Downham

Rainbow Land

R ainbows, rainbows, such a good thing!
A nd some people I've heard, make them want to sing.
I n your heart, you're filled with joy,
N ever a better feeling, boy oh boy!
B odies filled with a great power,
O nly a feeling where you don't want to cower.
W ater and sun, a perfect combination,

L oving others, a great celebration.
A fter a while, you'll feel hypnotised,
N ow if you don't believe me, you'll be surprised.
D angers, fears, you won't remember, after a day with the rainbow sender!

Ryan Johnson (8)
Downderry Primary School, Downham

Underwaterpus

In Underwaterpus,
Everybody shush! - Everybody cuss!
It's so calm and quiet,
There's hardly any riot.

The jolly jellyfish,
And the sparkly starfish.
The electric eel
And the southern seal.

Shoals of fish flutter by,
Never stopping to pry,
While lobsters carefully crawl
So they do not fall.

Aquatic plants always flourish,
So everything stays nourished.
From tiny-teeny plankton,
To big, boisterous salmon.

It's so great here,
Come and join us this year

In this underwater place,
Where everything's ace!
Aayushi Shrestha (9)
Downderry Primary School, Downham

The Land Of Love

In this world of wonder,
there is no such thing as hate.
But only love and equality,
a heartfelt place to escape.

With things to treat your sweet tooth,
everywhere you turn,
as rivers as sweet as chocolate,
your taste buds are sure to turn!

When in this kingdom
there is nothing to bring you down.
No failure,
nothing to cause a frown.

It's a view of colour,
a breeze of happiness floats through the air.
The sun is constantly burning brightly.
Any visitors will endlessly stare.

Evie Kielthy (11)
Downderry Primary School, Downham

Beneath The Waves

Beneath the waves stay many creatures,
Some are boring, but some have cool features,
Some have fins but some have claws,
While other ferocious animals
Have razor-sharp jaws,
Under the sea is where they can be.

Beneath the waves stay many plants,
Some are prickly, but some of them aren't,
Some have petals, but some have thorns,
While others have leaves that are shaped like horns,
Under the sea is where they can be.

Bishman Karnan (11)
Downderry Primary School, Downham

Candy City

In Candy City
it is always pretty.
It's full of lollipops
and Starburst pops.

Yummy Snickers
make it flicker.
Tasty Dairy Milk
are not made out of silk.

If you look at the stars
they're full of chocolate bars.
Come to this place
so you can have a taste.

Asmitha Thayaruban (7)
Downderry Primary School, Downham

Candy Land

C andy is delicious for people who are nice.
A river made out of caramel and popcorn is amazing.
N aughty children have marshmallows and Skittles every day.
D elicious gummy snakes appear to chase you when you eat them.
Y ummy toffee in a present falling out of a sleigh.

L ovely cola fizz spreading everywhere from a fountain.
A t the tasty, candy house there are lots of sweets to taste.
N aughty people do their homework, just for sweets.
D elightful adults don't eat sweets because they are unhealthy.

Filipe Papadopoulos (8)
Eastry CE Primary School, Eastry

Candy World

Candyfloss is very sweet,
a chocolate river can be a treat,
swirly lollies are all scrummy,
toffee helicopters, uum... they're very yummy,
cola bottles are funny and runny,
and also very scrummy.
Marshmallows can be very sticky
and you might even be a bit picky!
Gingerbread houses crumble and stumble,
they also make your tummy rumble,
candy canes are nice and crunchy,
popcorn is lovely and can be munchy,
Having cream... that's just scrumptious.
Gummy bears are the best and are delicious.

Imogen Elizabeth Cork (9)
Eastry CE Primary School, Eastry

Sport City

As messy as the football player Messi.
As muddy as Max my brother.
As serious as a snake.
As furious to win a match as my dad.
As strong as Hulk.
As famous as Taylor Swift.
As cool as a cucumber.
As fun as football.
As loud as a football ref.
As funny as a clown.
As sweaty as Ronaldo.
As fast as Flash.
As fit as a boxer.
As cheeky as a cheetah.
As sneaky as a snake.
As energetic as my friend Evie.
As focused as Santa Claus.
As active as aliens.

Grace Lauren Welch (9)
Eastry CE Primary School, Eastry

Halloween World

It is a terrifying terror
with wild witches and
frustrated Frankensteins.
Surrounded by bloodsucking bats
weird body pumpkins,
wetting the ground.
Monstrous trees trampling on panting pumpkins
and zigzagging zombies on the move.
Trying to get away from vicious vampires,
with shaking skeletons and gangling ghosts
with ghost gauntlets...

And they are all coming for you now!

Aidan Booth (9)
Eastry CE Primary School, Eastry

Nightmare Land

N aughty snakes poison people.
I hate monsters that sneak under people's beds at night.
G houls and gruesome ghosts make me shiver.
H elp, get me away!
T errifying clowns chase me about.
M onsters creep me out.
A ll vampires suck.
R ed snakes bite me and hurt.
E nter if you dare.
S ave me from the ghosts!

Harry Boakes (9)
Eastry CE Primary School, Eastry

Minecraft World

M inecraft makes you laugh.
I n Minecraft you build.
N ice Minecraft in front of your face.
E nd of the world.
C raft of the world.
R aft man.
A fter craft man!
F ast draft.
T idy craft.

W orld craft.
O f a craft.
R eal craft.
L ittle world.
D ig world.

Rhys Bagshaw (9)
Eastry CE Primary School, Eastry

Friend Island

On Friend Island, where Jennifer rules,
you will find evil Barbie dolls!
They are everywhere!
Oh, something else,
they are always watching you,
but on the other half of the island
it is beautiful and cute.
They have unicorns, blob walkers,
candy worms and more.
Another thing about the Barbies;
they are friends with each other,
but no one else.

Callum Roberts (9)
Eastry CE Primary School, Eastry

Evil Nightmare

N ight is the time we go to bed.
I t's chilly at night because it's dark.
G irls and boys scared at 3am.
H appy kids playing a game.
T ell my mum I had a deadly nightmare.
M y mum said, "Go back to bed!"
A ny dream will do.
R eady to get scared?
E vil nightmare comes for you.

Logan Moor (9)
Eastry CE Primary School, Eastry

Candy Crush

C andy is so sweet.
A nyone can eat.
N othing is new.
D on't you think so too?
Y ou need to share.

C andy needs some care.
R hubarb is so great.
U nder the clouds you wouldn't want to wait.
S omeone is getting fat.
H ave they fed their cat?

Flynn Goodrich (8)
Eastry CE Primary School, Eastry

Food, Food, Food!

Fun buns, jolly lollies, runny honey.
Not forgetting the chocolate money!

Jelly wellies, strawberry laces.
Fascinating faces, chicken legs and lots of eggs!

Roast beef that's full of grief,
Sticky lollies, yummy gummies.

And lots of jelly tots too!

Oliver Regan (9)
Eastry CE Primary School, Eastry

Music Mayhem

The glorious guitar playing under bright lights,
beating drums are the children's favourite thing.
The bass is not really a disgrace.
Here's some instruments not for me;
Tuba, trumpet, recorder, cello, saxophone
and not the piano.
No, no, no!

Freddie Silk (9)
Eastry CE Primary School, Eastry

Army Base

A rmy base.
R etreat in the helicopters.
M arching on parade.
Y ou can do it!

B ridge bomber.
A irbase.
S ergeant shouts.
E xciting mission - that is the army way.

George Clarke (8)
Eastry CE Primary School, Eastry

Halloween Land

I hear a cruel witch cackling.
I smell burning smoke from the candles.
I see scary ghosts everywhere.
I touch vicious spiders on my wall.
I taste delicious sweets from my Halloween bag
And watch out for the magical witches!

Joshua Kemp (9)
Eastry CE Primary School, Eastry

Fast Food

F erocious flavour.
A gonising apples.
S alty snails.
T errific tea.

F antastic fruits.
O utrageous omelettes.
O ozy olives.
D isturbing dates.

James Baker (8)
Eastry CE Primary School, Eastry

Sweet Food City

Sweet Food City
is so very sticky
with caramel chocolate
and Nutella sides.

There're monkeys who suck candy
that are so very sandy
and there is Turkish delight
which can shine very bright.

It's Sweet Food City galore
and is open for all.
There are candyfloss mountains
flowing with lemonade fountains.

Open the door
and find yourself in...
Sweet Food City!

Jeremiah Taylor (10)
Edgebury Primary School, Chislehurst

Butterflies

Butterflies can be blue, green, yellow or red.
Swiftly fluttering above my head.
Caterpillar to chrysalis, sprouting from their house.
Smaller than an acorn, smaller than a mouse.
Fluttering through the trees, fluttering through the flowers.
I don't know about you, but I could watch them for hours.
Butterflies only have seven days to fly.
Sadly, then we might have to say bye-bye.

Rose Acutt (9)
Edgebury Primary School, Chislehurst

Snowglobe

S anta's here delivering presents.
N obody knows what they going to get
O n Christmas Day.
W ell, you'll just have to wait and see!
G oing along the icy roads
L eaping around like there's no doubt.
O h well, it's Christmas!
B e as happy as you can be.
E verlasting fun and games.

Erin Cole (10)
Edgebury Primary School, Chislehurst

Down In Candy Land

In Candy Land, the pink unicorn puffed up her hair,
but no one knows where.
With the lollipops dares,
everybody is scared.
Down through the dark chocolate park,
cookie children pull everything apart.
This is Candy Land,
I hope your time was grand!

Megan Smart (9)
Edgebury Primary School, Chislehurst

Minecraft

M y poem.
I deas.
N ever stop dreaming.
E verlasting magic.
C reativity.
R hyme.
A crostic.
F acts.
T ake your imagination to another world!

Evie Kouzaris (10)
Edgebury Primary School, Chislehurst

Candy Land

Up in Candy City
not everything you find is pretty.
Don't forget, when you leave
you're always welcome back.
What's your favourite sweet?
Is it a blackjack?
There's no jobs to complete,
oh isn't that sweet?
There's so many things to make,
don't forget to try the vanilla milkshake.
There's so many sweet cakes to try,
oh and don't forget the brambly pie.

Peggy Julia Barrett (9)
Finberry Primary School, Ashford

Underwater

U nderwater is pretty.
N ow I like to eat fish.
D eep in the sea is very dark.
E very fish is beautiful.
R ivers lead to the sea.
W hales swim in the dark sea.
A ll the fish swim in schools.
T he most fierce is a shark.
E veryone is scared of sharks.
R ainbow-coloured fish are my fave!

Maggie Mae McQuillan (8)
Finberry Primary School, Ashford

Magical Land

M agic Land is always fun in every way
A nd everyone has a magical property
G oing to places on flying brooms
I ncluding every flavour water and trees
C ellars always happened to sing
A nd everything is great, just you wait.
L and itself will form a wish with one flick of a wand.

Jessica Slade (9)
Finberry Primary School, Ashford

Friend Land

In Friend Land we love hugs
and the favourite dog is a pug
the favourite name is Doug.

We like to play
on a sunny day.
Everyone likes you
even when you shout boo!

There is a friendship tree
and smiles are free.
Friend Land is great
there is no such thing as hate.

Adra Louise Rothwell
Finberry Primary School, Ashford

Candy Land

A long time ago, when the earth was green
and everything was free,
there lived a unicorn called Bree.
Her eyes were bright
and she rode in Candy Land,
she sat on a slide,
it was made of candy,
because she liked sugar candy!

Jonathan Osho (9)
Finberry Primary School, Ashford

Forest

F orests are huge and noisy.
O ak woods are there.
R ivers are nearby.
E verywhere around for you.
S teak and other stuff to eat.
T ime for you to pick.

Timotei Bilc (9)
Finberry Primary School, Ashford

Sandy Beach

B eautiful, white, orange sand.
E pic, blue, strong, wet waves.
A mazing, big, windy view.
C rabs scuttle along the sand.
H ave lots of fun!

Noah Foy (9)
Finberry Primary School, Ashford

Rocks

R ocks are made by tremors.
O ld rocks may have fossils.
C aves are dark, rocky and scary.
K ick the boulder off the mountain.
S now is on Mount Everest.

Bethany Venn (8)
Fleetdown Primary School, Dartford

Dream Land

Lying on the floor, twinkling stars from the nightlight on the ceiling,
I start to drift off with that dreamy feeling.
My eyelids feel heavy
and then comes sweet slumber,
taking me to dreamland and dancing the rumba!

Everybody is welcome in Dream Land,
although some terms and conditions apply.
The sun shines and you just have to be happy as the time flies by.
Make merry in this land of dreams and party on,
when you're ready, click your fingers
and you'll be gone!

When there, if you spy the river, far and low,
here will appear a magical rainbow.
Reach the edge of the river
and crave something sweet,
a few words from your tongue
and a chocolate waterfall you shall meet.
In Dreamland, your imagination will rule
and the rules of the journey will apply to all!

Iona Trigg (9)
Hamstreet Primary Academy, Ashford

Candy Life

The chocolate, candyfloss mortar,
children running through the streets,
pick a gummy bear from a tree,
every hour Skittles fall,
everybody starts to drool.

Go in a pub, they offer you a drink,
say yes, chocolate comes from the sink.
When it is autumn,
Ferrero Rocher fall from trees.

People go rafting, they take spoons,
not to paddle, to get that chocolatey cream!
The train brakes are strawberry laces,
clouds are whipped cream.

There is a sport in Candy Town,
people travel from far and wide,
the sport's chocolate surfing!
Bushes made out of candyfloss,
but there's a whole world out there
and you've only seen mine!

Rhys Jones (9)
Hamstreet Primary Academy, Ashford

A Chocolate Land!

A chocolate land I stumbled upon,
Where all the greenery had magically gone.
The fields were chocolate, the mountains alike,
I had the urgency to take a big bite.
Yummy, yummy in my tummy,
This chocolate was so very scrummy.
The river flowing before me,
Was chocolate in all its full glory.
There was a big slide,
I climbed a ladder to try.
I slid faster and faster and could not slow down,
And as I came to a bend,
I could suddenly see the end.
"Hooray!" I shouted, as I finally sped,
Into that chocolate river,
Which went over my head.
I took a big gasp and came up to the top
And then I went and drank the lot!

Zach William Rivett (9)
Hamstreet Primary Academy, Ashford

My Musical Mayhem World

In my world, it's loud and lovable
In my world, it's filled with music madness
My world is the best, beautiful land

There is music all around
There is noise on every street
My world is the party planet you want to be on

There's also a party princess in our world
She is crazy and she has a kind heart. Stop
This is a Princess you would like to meet

Now I need to warn you about our enemy, *Noise!*
Noise is the most annoying person in the Milky Way
He is the complete opposite of music.
He has wasps for minions by the way.

PS: he has wasps because of their noisiness.

Megan Pettit (9)
Hamstreet Primary Academy, Ashford

Candy Land

Candy is handy when you want a snack
My favourite is liquorice because it is black
When my happiness needs a helping hand
I take a trip to my favourite place, Candy Land!

In place of sand is sherbet
In place of bricks is nougat
This makes a very sweet house for you and your spouse

There are lollipop flowers that give you superpowers
that keeps you happy for hours and hours
The strawberry laces put smiles on faces
the marshmallow mountains are one of my favourite places

All children should come and visit Candy Land but I'm afraid parents are banned!

Isla Jones (9)
Hamstreet Primary Academy, Ashford

Football In Space

On the moon, there was a big boom, aliens and humans.
There was a man called Bert,
who got very hurt,
as the aliens brushed dirt on him.
As the teams were ready,
someone ate some beans and it stank!

The game started, then the referee farted,
a man shouted, "This is bonzer!"
Then spilled his Fanta.

It was a draw till the aliens came
and then a fraction of the game was left.
As the ball was kicked into a wall hard,
an alien got a red card,
and his manager put him to bed with his ted!

Alex Tomlinson (9)
Hamstreet Primary Academy, Ashford

Places Wonderful

Music City is my favourite place,
with lots of drums and lots of bass,
with lots of guitars and singing galore,
and lots of people on the dance floor.

Animal Land is a place of wonder and happiness,
and a place with no darkness,
all the cute animals like to be wild and free,
so if you're an animal,
this is the place you want to be.

If you like your sport, comes to Sport Side,
you can do any sport you decide,
they are all quite competitive here,
so be very careful dear.

Ríona O'Neill (9)
Hamstreet Primary Academy, Ashford

The Magic Land

The bushes are soft and fluffy,
made from sweet candyfloss
with a sparkly gloss.

The tuneful piano bridge,
made from creamy chocolate out of the fridge,
lollies on the edge,
by the hedge.

See-through, like glass,
green grass of jelly beans,
eaten by all the teens.

Snow bites falling down,
snow and ice
nibbled by all the mice.

Falling softly into the cola river,
the yummy lime leaves
magicked a drink, sure to make you pleased.

Erin Eccles-Shorter (9)
Hamstreet Primary Academy, Ashford

The Candy Land

This poem is about a little, cute man,
who turned into a gingerbread man.
He was lost,
nowhere to go,
no one had seen him,
nowhere at all.

He did what he knew,
he said he would make a soup.
A soup of what? A gingerbread man?
Then out of nowhere,
a stick came out and guess what?
It was a chocolate stick.

They were sweet friends,
as always to be,
they made a cute home,
and loved it forever.

Natalia Andreea Dragomir (9)
Hamstreet Primary Academy, Ashford

Music Land

Music Land is a happy place
Everyone has a smiley face
The sun is a huge, shiny CD
Which glows and sends great tunes to me.

Birds don't tweet, they simply hum
Every window looks like a drum
Musical notes instead of trees
Gently swaying in the breeze.

A keyboard instead of the path
I jump on the notes and it makes me laugh!
Guitar-shaped clouds above my head
A lullaby when I go to bed!

Erin Othen (9)
Hamstreet Primary Academy, Ashford

The Underwater Goal

Goal!
What a strike!
Do I need to say the name?
No, because it's Harry Kane.

As bubbles rise,
the game goes on,
although the referee might need to stop,
because he has had too many pies.

As the game draws to a close,
the bubbles go up the goalkeeper's nose.
The referee blows the full-time whistle,
the players are off as fast as the referee drives his tiny little Renault Twingo.

Fraser Henderson (9)
Hamstreet Primary Academy, Ashford

Wolves

On the quiet mountain summit my pack lies.
I am one of them.
I feel the warmth of the summer sun on my fur.
What could disturb the peace of this day?
I head down the stream, where the water is cold and fresh.
Shadows lurk in the dark woodland.
A herd of deer? Or hunters?
Camouflage clothes? Or leaves and branches?
Then a shot.
Bang!
I run.
I run away.
Who has survived?

Matthew Baggaley (9)
Hamstreet Primary Academy, Ashford

Dessert Land

Come and visit my land,
it's made of biscuits and sweets,
the floors are made of marzipan,
the trees are chocolate logs.

Come and visit my land,
it's made of chocolate and cake,
the beds are made of marshmallow,
the walls are gingerbread.

Come and visit my land,
it's made of desserts galore,
so if you've got a sweet tooth,
come and eat some more!

Matilda Glancy (9)
Hamstreet Primary Academy, Ashford

Animals

A nimals roam freely, exploring this extraordinary island.
N ot like any other island, this one is one of a kind.
I ncredible animals fill this island.
M an is only allowed in to help and take care of the animals.
A ll of the animals are happy and treated with care.
L ove and listen to your animals.
S oft as cotton wool, their beds are so welcoming.

Lucy Maddison (9)
Hamstreet Primary Academy, Ashford

Awesome Ed

Every day is magical in my world.

In the morning I wake up
and I talk to the sun.
I go downstairs
and I get a gift from my mom.

Upon the rainbow
the sacred unicorn stood right there,
with the wind blowing through her flawless,
glistening hair.

You may be thinking, who is the main character?
It is Ed, with messy clothes,
but he has an awesome pose!

Oscar Grant (9)
Hamstreet Primary Academy, Ashford

Fantasy

Unicorns roam in the magical meadow,
mermaids laze in the lagoon so mellow,
Pegasus' soar through fluffy white clouds.

Fairies, elves and dwarves make the most of the mood,
Centaurs are royalty, they rule the land with dignity and grace,
everyone lives in peace and harmony, no war, no hate.

If you believe then you will see
this magical world of fantasy.

Lilly Santer (9)
Hamstreet Primary Academy, Ashford

The Dark Shadow

I hear children scream as I hide in cellar,
I smell decaying flesh lying on the ground.
I find bones and bloodstains
everywhere on the floor,
I feel filthy, damp walls crumbling on me.
I starve in agony, not daring to come out,
I watch people perish one by one.
I see a shadow looming down the road,
disappearing into a house.
Will it ever stop?

Ben Smith (9)
Hamstreet Primary Academy, Ashford

Candy Land

Welcome to Candy Land,
the candy canes bash like a band.
There is a crunchy floor
and lots to explore.
Smarties floating in the air,
try and catch one if you dare.
As tall as houses, there are chocolate trees,
but if you want anything you have to say please.
The candyfloss bushes are bright pink,
be very careful or you might sink!

Grace Praman (9)
Hamstreet Primary Academy, Ashford

Circus Land

C ircus Land is fun,
I t is the best place to be.
R est or run,
C ircus Land has something for you.
U nbelievably real,
S till there in your imagination.

L augh or cry
A nd stare at the sky.
N ot for the faint-hearted,
D isappointment, you will not feel.

Lily Smith (9)
Hamstreet Primary Academy, Ashford

Candy Land

In Candy Land
there's a chocolate band.
I have a friend that's food
called Donut Dude.

This is the place
where you can stuff your face.
But watch Big Ben
when it strikes ten.

Just come right here
where you can drink beer.
Just come right in,
but don't eat from a bin...

Jaden Bailey Blunsdon (9)
Hamstreet Primary Academy, Ashford

Quackland Band

Well, I'm a duck
I'm covered in muck.
I did a quack
then scratched my back.

My name is Jack
and I quack.
I'm in a band
a Quack Land band.

I play guitar
and travel far
to do my quacking concert
and whatever I do
I just knew
I was going to be famous one day!

Tom Dickens (10)
Hamstreet Primary Academy, Ashford

Sugar Land

Under the trees of candyfloss, unicorns sleep.
New candy flowers bud and grow.
I think this world is unique in its own way.
Come into this glittery, edible town
Of colourful, shiny gingerbread houses.
Ruled by the animals and mermaids of lemonade rivers.
No one knows how the magic happens.

Sophie Eliza Ward (9)
Hamstreet Primary Academy, Ashford

My Majestic Musical Land

M y land is made of music.
U nderneath the starry sky.
S ounds of drums beating and people singing stand out from the bass playing.
I go to cello school, where I learned to perform.
C ello, my favourite instrument; easier to play relaxing music at end of day.

Michaiah Asare (9)
Hamstreet Primary Academy, Ashford

Sport! Football Forever

S tadiums full of cheering fans!
P layers giving their everything to win!
O ver the wall and past the goalie.
R ight past the defenders.
T ime's up! The whistle blows, we won!

Harry Body (9)
Hamstreet Primary Academy, Ashford

Sweets

C andyland is fun and exciting.
A lways stuff your face.
N othing is inedible.
D iets are illegal.
Y ou can eat everything!

Jay Russell (9)
Hamstreet Primary Academy, Ashford

Mythical Mountain

Mythical Mountain is a magical place
Where mythical creatures fly all over the place.
The griffins and Pegasuses race in the clear air,
While the ferocious dragons sleep in their gloomy, treasure-filled lair.

The unicorns and alicorns test their magic up high;
As the griffins go soaring through the light-blue sky.
The unicorns and alicorns travel in the mythical train,
As the dragons go flying in the mythical 'Express' plane.

Above the clouds lies the most epic place of all myths,
the Mythical Mountain city on top of the cliffs;
its beauty captures your attention best in the night,
especially the wonders of its colourful glowing light.
Mythical Mountain is the most magical place you will ever know!

Naomi Akpomuje (10)
Hextable Primary School, Hextable

Fantasy Land: The World Of Books

Books are magical, books are your life
Books will create your new, loving wife.
Listen to this poem to let your imagination run wild
Don't worry, this place is mild.

Fantasy Land, the world of books
This land has a book called Crooks.
The books have wonderful stories that lurk inside
There is not one single place where they can hide.

Cinderella, the Wizard of Oz, Matilda too
But don't forget Winnie the Pooh.
Jack and the Beanstalk, David Walliams too
Diary of a Wimpy Kid, the whole series for you!

There is no boring and blaring TV
That makes your eyes too weepy to see.
The BFG stands for Big Friendly Giant.
With this guy, this place is silent.

There are no electronic gadgets about.
Not even one person is tough or will shout.

Books could create a loyal friend.
In this world, your life will never end.

Scarlett Davie (9)
Hextable Primary School, Hextable

DDLC

Entering my name in this wonderful game.
Silly names in this game.
Four amazing girls, one out of my league.
Athletic, beautiful, popular.
One's called Sayori
A childhood friend.
She goes crazy!
Round the bend!
Natsuki, a cute girl
With a sour attitude.
Nowhere near being subdued.
Yuri, timid girl
Finds comfort in the world of books.
She has elegant looks.
Last but not least, Monika
The president of this club.
She loves hugs.
Now I'm forced into this club by Sayori.
I sold my soul for a cupcake that day
That Natsuki made!

Now Monika is messing with the game
It's basically for fame.
Writing poems every night
It's time to do what's right!
But, these girls are in the wrong timeline...

Chloe Green (9)
Hextable Primary School, Hextable

Candy Land

Mouthwatering, jaw-dropping, that's what food is.
If you want food, then come to
Candy Land for a Twix.
If you always have pizza and you say you're done
Then come here for a taste of our love.

Candy cows, sugar spiders, there is so much more.
Popcorn pigs, edible elephants, lollipop llamas too.
It's candy galore, so much more for you.

Chocolate chip cookies, trampolines, candyfloss trees to love.
You would say it's heavenly and say it comes from above.
Houses made of gingerbread, rivers with vanilla milk.
The candyfloss holders are made from soft silk.

The sun is made from a lollipop, as tasty as waffles.
Whenever anyone comes here, the waffles are all gobbled!

Emelia Anne Steele (10)
Hextable Primary School, Hextable

My Candy Pixel World

Welcome to the candy world.
Clouds are light candyfloss.
Ice cream River, sprinkle grass
And the pixel creatures land.
The world is really, really huge
And it smells like beautiful vanilla.
We can hear animals sing
Birds, rabbits make their song
And they're singing all night long.
All day there is a doughnut sun
But at night it's like a white cake bun.
On the land is chocolate wood
And lollipop flowers, the best food.
Creatures live in chocolate houses
Small as a toy.
Yes, this land is in one look!

Alicja Jolanta Lechowicz (10)
Hextable Primary School, Hextable

Turquoise Candy Reef

The glamorous ocean
Is where fish make potions
Under the ocean
Where people don't wear lotion.

On the path.
Lies a rainbow raft.
Everyone is sweet
And we always have a treat.

The grass is made of strawberry laces
Where you can stuff your faces.
It smells like candy underwater
The mermaid Queen has a flawless daughter!

Everything is edible.
The trees are flexible.

Near the ancient cave
Where everyone is afraid
Lies the golden treasure mound
Never to be found.

So come visit this place.
Just don't go near the cave!

Evie Whitlock Wilcox (9)
Hextable Primary School, Hextable

Ghoul City

The ghouls think they're too cool for school.
They live in a grey world,
and they will take you in a whirl.
They're rapidly fast,
and they will send you to the past.
Their favourite food is brain burger.
When you see them, you're going to fall.
When you go to the Hall of death
it has booby-traps.
They are all over the place like a map.
They're scary, like Bloody Mary!
They look grey, filled with scares
and they will give you nightmares!
Full of smoke, never have they spoke.

Lis Abdullahu (10)
Hextable Primary School, Hextable

Dunkin' Donuts

Unbelievably baked to perfection doughnuts
Try our new flavoured coconuts
Strawberry, chocolate, vanilla sauce.
It's all incredibly delicious, of course.

My fluffy, cotton candy clouds
Carry cute, little baby whales.
All the way to the chocolate river,
the gummy snakes can also slither.

Raining lollipops all the time.
The green ones taste like fantastic lime.
Doughnuts, yummy doughnuts, they are the best,
But I've eaten them, there's none left!

Mia Penny (10)
Hextable Primary School, Hextable

Sleepy Land

As its majestic leaves dance across the wavy, frazzled bushes,
the powerful wind whistles through the hollow tree trunks.
Crystal clear water bolts over the smooth pebbles,
the fluffy clouds are as soft as a baby's bum.
Whoosh goes the breeze as it brushes upon my face,
you can hear the hammock swinging to the calming music box.
The sunset melts over the gasping view
as I take a seat on the relaxing beanbags.
I flutter my eyelids
and I start to softly snore.

Nell Regan (10)
Hextable Primary School, Hextable

Underwater Candy Land

This is a place that is very pretty,
that's a very bubbly Undercity.
Come along, have some fun
join in with everyone.

There are lollipops for you to lick,
chocolate drips on your candy sticks,
liquorice swaying like a candy tree.

Colourful milkshakes, cookies too,
beautiful unicorn saying, "I love you!"

Tasty candy canes just for you,
boiled sweets, yummy too.
Yummy, yummy chocolate soup,
icky, sticky, yummy gum.

Louisa Collins (10)
Hextable Primary School, Hextable

Book Bay

In brilliant Book Bay, it's light,
Because of the stars that shine bright.

Cosy cushions as a path
and a tent as big as five baths.

An adventurous bookshelf
with books for health.

Non-fiction books are always right,
scary books that look like they bite.

Fairy tales for you to love
and romantic books with sparkly doves.

The fluffy tent is super warm,
also, no books are torn.

Just relax and read!

Elouise Sophie Waterton (10)
Hextable Primary School, Hextable

No-Man's-Land WWII

War is a day of gore
You wouldn't believe what I saw.
We sent out an English spy
I saw a grey, foggy gas in the sky.
They've taken over most of No-Man's-Land
but together, we will always stand.
I never see the big, bright sun
but I will always see my loaded machine gun.
I see a soldier who is dead
When my life flashes past, I see my bed.
I shall always remember, I love my wife
But I'm sad I risked my poor, little life.

Alex Hills (9)
Hextable Primary School, Hextable

Chocolate Land

Chocolate is my new love
Ferrero Rocher are my life.
It is as delicious as chocolate ice cream on top of a wonderful waffle
No one will think this place is terribly awful.
While chocolate trickles down your throat
Just like you riding on a gorgeous candy cane boat.
It is so colourful, it makes my clear eyes burn
It makes your focus in mind turn.
The grass rains Maltesers up to the sky
Once you've gobbled up one, it will make you fly high!

Maisie Olivia Brown (9)
Hextable Primary School, Hextable

Candy Town

In Candy Town
everything's brown.
It's like a dream come true!
You can stuff your face,
there isn't one brick,
chocolate makes it stick!
It tastes so good,
there's nothing made of wood!
Look, there's the Candy Queen sitting in the pool,
trying to act all cool!
The land is so pretty,
when I walk around, it makes me dizzy.
It's so beautiful, you can see rainbows,
it's a magical place here!

Olivia Paige Stoyles (10)
Hextable Primary School, Hextable

Marshmallow Mountain

On Marshmallow Mountain, everything glows,
There are gummy rivers that have a rhythmic flow,
Marshmallow people live in every single street,
Hoping to buy all kinds of sweets.
There are candy cane trees with lollipop leaves,
And a chocolate gym with marshmallow people who heave,
A gingerbread house levitated by a flying saucer,
With an ice cream elephant whose ears outgrew a horse,
As well as living gummy bears running a marathon course!

Fiona Grace Horley (9)
Hextable Primary School, Hextable

Candy Land

In my dreams
stars are bright, colourful starbursts,
lollipops waved to the tune of the winds,
the brown chocolate lake
sends ripples to the shore.
Skittles explode, *bang!* - form a rainbow,
candy canes shine like a splash of gold.
The moon, a gummy banana, bright and bold,
a gingerbread house stood tall and proud,
surrounded by an enormous crowd.
That's the magic of Candy Land!

Jack Hillam (10)
Hextable Primary School, Hextable

Candy Code

In Candy Code
there's no normal mode.
There's a chocolate lake
filled with long, gummy snakes.
It's a colourful city
so very, very pretty.
The grass is gummy bears,
but no one cares.
We eat it all day,
after we eat, we go and play.
Lollipops are sweet
but chocolate is my treat.
Please come and visit this place,
it's a place where you can stuff your face.

Sophia Stanton (9)
Hextable Primary School, Hextable

Winter Wonderland

Winter Wonderland is a magical place.
It puts a smile upon your face.
See houses thick with snow.
It's Winter Wonderland, don't you know?

With Santa's sleigh zooming around the sky.
See the stars twinkle way up high.
You hear the reindeer prance around.
Prance, Dancer and Vixen too.

That is the magic, come and see.
I'm sure you will be glad, believe me!

Dolcie Olivia Mae Couldridge (9)
Hextable Primary School, Hextable

Sugar Rush City

Sugar Rush City is the best
It's better than the rest.
Sugar Rush is delightful
But the gummy bears are frightful.
The rainbow is colourful
The chocolate river is wonderful.
The gummy bears are puffy
The candyfloss trees are fluffy.
The lollipops bloom
The cloud sometimes go *boom*.
The cloud went *boom* one day
and suddenly there was no candy left!

Bridget Hancock (10)
Hextable Primary School, Hextable

Kitty City

Everything is pretty
in Kitty City.
The Kitty Queen
loves glitter cream.

There's lots of bees
flying around gummy bear trees
Near the Harribo Cafe,
they serve créme bruleé.

Everything that goes into their tummy is very yummy,
they perform puppet shows which are rather funny.
So come and visit this place
where you can stuff your face!

Amy Morley (10)
Hextable Primary School, Hextable

Magic Land

M agic every day.
A nts walk into scenes of wonderful pictures.
G iants stomp around all day.
I guanas all cheer as the great wizard does a trick.
C ows talk too much all day.

L ollipops have eyes and can see you.
A pples stick to the floor.
N ow it is time for the animals to go to bed.
D oves say, "Goodbye."

Bradley Archer (10)
Hextable Primary School, Hextable

Dream Land

Delightful Dream Land
there is no slippy sand,
It really is quite great
it's never in a super state.

It's always surprisingly pretty
in this vast, busy city.
We welcome friendly cats and small bats
and some nervous rats.

Everyone is kind
when they make up their creative mind.
Your special dreams always come true
if you can count up to two.

Lauren Bonnie Sawkings (9)
Hextable Primary School, Hextable

Candy Land

Candy has a delicious taste,
lots of candy goes to waste.
I love yummy, colourful gumdrops,
but the best are swirly, whirly lollipops.
My brother says Haribos are his favourite sweets,
but I love rainbow Sour Skittles as my treat.
The trees are bright green
and they're all filled with whipped cream.
The roads are made of jelly
and sometimes it ends up in my belly.

Maddie Vesey (9)
Hextable Primary School, Hextable

Unicorn Land

Unicorn Land is magical as a magical gem.
In this land there is an area to chill.
Your world of poetry begins.
It's a world of lights to show.
You can have a bite of sparkles to know.
The unicorns are as glorious as glitter.
They're all a magical and colourful lot.
Their horns are as sharp as a piece of thorn.
Unicorn Land is as incredible as a milkshake!

Millie Thompson (9)
Hextable Primary School, Hextable

Candy Land

I live in Candy Land,
where there is no sand.
It tastes so good
and there is no wood,
instead, there is jelly,
which is very smelly.

The path's made of chocolate,
it tastes so good,
that I hide it in my hood.
My brother's favourite sweets are Haribos
and my favourite sweets
are sour sweets as my treat.
I love Candy Land!

Harrison Jacob Pyle (10)
Hextable Primary School, Hextable

Fortnite Land

Tilted towers
have lots of flowers.
I tried to get some powers.
If you build,
you might get killed.

In salty springs
there's no hot wings,
but you can get lots of things.

Junk junction
has a lot of junk.
I call everyone a punk.

Shifty shafts
has lots of parts,
but I don't like to wear their scarves.

Jack Nurthen (9)
Hextable Primary School, Hextable

War Land

Tea's on the floor, like a river flowing after a hundred years.
The blood is rising.
No one likes the sound of death.
People crying in the street.
Hitler not budging.
Heavy lugging, so much equipment.
Booming, stopping.
Hitler losing.
Guns come to a draw.
People stop crying.
Country celebrating.
People shouting, "We won!"

Connor Martin George Bishop (10)
Hextable Primary School, Hextable

No-Man's-Land

A time of warfare.
A time of despair.
A time of hostile people.
A time of war that is lethal.
A time of soldiers risking their lives.
A time of nasty knives.
A time of putrid gases.
A time of armies amassing.
A time of deadly warfare.
A time of nightmares.
There the soldiers lie in Flanders Field
That we will always remember.

Archie Carroll (9)
Hextable Primary School, Hextable

Necropolis

N ever-ending death.
E ternal torture.
C ruelty to all.
R eaping their souls.
O ne million of the dead, oblivious to life.
P oor people peeling away from home.
O n the torture machines, blood is shed.
L ike the end of days.
I n the land of the dead.
S ouls screaming to leave.

Toby Cockerham (10)
Hextable Primary School, Hextable

Foodandy Land

In Foodandy Land
everything is grand.
Delicious cream
comes with dreams.

Not one brick,
not one stick.
What a pretty land
no speck of sand.

Swirling, slithering spaghetti in a jar,
delicious, marvellous meatballs there are.
Scrumptious, crunchy chocolate right here,
peaceful, relaxed place it is!

Happy Grace Chikerema (9)
Hextable Primary School, Hextable

Candy Crush

When candy came in different colours
it tasted like cold ice cream.
When the candy canes danced in the whirling wind
candy was a beautiful flower.
When you ate them, it gave you power!
When I saw Candy Crush, I began to rush.
The candy was a sweet smell.
To get to Candy Crush, you ring a bell.
This is Candy Crush!

Oliver Moore (9)
Hextable Primary School, Hextable

Shimmer, Glitz And Sparkle

Emerald-green ballerina leaves, frantically pirrouetting.
This rapturous blissful land is no land for the indisposed and upsetting.
The gleaming, burnished rhinestones spill like rain, uncontrollably...
The scenic land is now a glamorous thought waiting to be heard -
When heard; a dream in a beauty sleep, not wanting to be disturbed.

Kelila Ogieva-Okunbor (10)
Hextable Primary School, Hextable

Pizza

Pizzas hit my head.
Pizzas are my bed.
The cheese grater is my tool.
Pizzas rule!
Pizzas are yum.
Pizzas are good in the sun.
Pizzas are the best.
Pizza is the only thing, I'll leave the rest!
Pizzas are a hit because they're lit!
Pizza is my lunch.
But I guess you could say it's brunch!

Joseph Bell (10)
Hextable Primary School, Hextable

Pokémon Rules!

Pokémon rules like a king.
Charmander is a fool of reckoning.
Ash is cool at school.

Pokémon rules as an overlord.
Lapras likes to explore.
Ash likes to eat mash!

Pokémon is like a king.
Butterfree likes to battle in a gym the shape of a wedding ring.
Ash now has to dash!

Noah Frederick Leland Dawson (9)
Hextable Primary School, Hextable

Frightening Forest

I hear the *tap, tap, tap* of the death beetle as it climbs the tree.
I see the brown bark as the tapping death beetle climbs up it.
I smell the dead animals, rotting through the forest.
I taste the rotting animals and the poison mix together.
I touched the rock-hard animals to take them to the bin.

Lily-Rose Bishop (10)
Hextable Primary School, Hextable

Welcome To Bouncing Kingdom!

My land is a gigantic trampoline!
You can hear energetic children laughing as loud as a lion.
You can feel the blizzard beneath your feet.
You can see everyone having more fun than they have ever had before.
You can taste the frozen air as you jump up to the wide sky.

I love jumping!

Charlotte Louise Sewell (10)
Hextable Primary School, Hextable

Under The Sea

The magical world
of Under The Sea,
as bright as the sun
and as pretty as the mermaid
that has lots of fun.
The magical world of Under The Sea,
where all the fishes play
and the jellyfish stay.
So come and explore
the magical world of Under The Sea.

Keira Leigh Farnham (10)
Hextable Primary School, Hextable

Anime World

Anime world is so cool.
They have an innumerable amount of pools.
For some people, it is hard to draw.
Their mansions are as big as the Queen's house.
Their entertainment is a running mouse.
They have their own servants for free
And a golden, shiny key.

Molly Chandler (10)
Hextable Primary School, Hextable

Reptilian Ruins

Reptilian ruins littered the land,
snakes to attention stand.
Tangled vines dropped from the sky,
long snakes scuttered by.
Tiny tree stumps getting my way,
hissing grass sways away.
Immense trees blocked my view,
scaly reptiles scare you!

Lenny John Lewis (9)
Hextable Primary School, Hextable

Untitled

C andy Land is made of scrumptious sweets.
A mazing action happens here.
N o fabulous fruits or vegetables, only cheer.
D o your thing, it's a land for everyone.
Y ou're welcome to my colourful Candy Land.

Leo Baker (9)
Hextable Primary School, Hextable

Cheese Land

C hunky Cheddar melting in my land.
H oles and yummy yellow.
E ating smelly cheese, crunch, crunch!
E dible, excellent cheese!
S oft as a baby's bottom.
E at cheese in my land!

Chloe Jones (10)
Hextable Primary School, Hextable

Fortnite Land

F abulous fantastic.
O nly one Fortnite Land.
R acing against time.
T ranquil.
N erves are calm.
I mportant to succeed.
T iny places.
E ager to win.

Herbie Holland (9)
Hextable Primary School, Hextable

Star Wars

S tormtroopers.
T errifying.
A ll the Jedi.
R eady for battle.

W ith all their weapons.
A ll Jedis.
R eady for battle.
S tart the battle!

Jacob Hick (9)
Hextable Primary School, Hextable

Candy Land

C hewing candy in my mouth.
A mazing, popping, scrumptious candy.
N othing is more exciting.
D elicious, tasty candy canes.
Y ummy food in their tummy.

Tommy Hibbert (9)
Hextable Primary School, Hextable

Football Land

A football land
is what I planned.
With different balls,
to fire into the wide goal.
Ronaldo, Messi, Zaha and Piqué
is the team I would like to play with!

Will Brazier (9)
Hextable Primary School, Hextable

Cracking Candy

C racking candy.
A dhesive chocolate river.
N aughty children being greedy.
D elicious sweets.
Y ummy sweets, so eat some.

Frankie Hibbert (9)
Hextable Primary School, Hextable

YOUNG WRITERS INFORMATION

We hope you have enjoyed reading this book – and that you will continue to in the coming years.

If you're a young writer who enjoys reading and creative writing, or the parent of an enthusiastic poet or story writer, do visit our website **www.youngwriters.co.uk**. Here you will find free competitions, workshops and games, as well as recommended reads, a poetry glossary and our blog.

If you would like to order further copies of this book, or any of our other titles, then please give us a call or visit **www.youngwriters.co.uk**.

Young Writers
Remus House
Coltsfoot Drive
Peterborough
PE2 9BF
(01733) 890066
info@youngwriters.co.uk